JOLLIE PUBLICATION PRESENTS

BEHIND A PRETTY SMILE

Anurag Mishra

First published by Jollie Publication 2022
Second Edition - June 2023

ACKNOWLEDGEMENT

Interior - Black and White

Author Name - Anurag Mishra

Type-writer - Ishu

Editor - Jollie Team

Publisher - Jollie Publication

FOREWORD

Anurag Mishra was born in 5th March 2007. Since his childhood he admired poets and poetry. As he grew up he developed his intrest in literature and started writing poetry. Apart from poetry he is interested in dance and art. His parents Mr. Santosh Mishra and Mrs. Priyanka Mishra encouraged and helped him at every point of his life, they taught him the importance of discipline in life. He is thankful to his guardians, well-wishers, friends and best friend, Mayank for supporting his interest in literature.

This book "Behind A Pretty Smile" portrays pain, suffering, tears, loneliness and nature. This book aims to showcase that behind a pretty smile there are many things that a person keeps within himself\herself. You can connect with the author -

Email - cuteanuragmishra4244@gmail.com

Instagram - @woeful_eyes_

Far From My Sight

You are just like a star,
I can see you, but you are too far.
Holding your cozy hand,
I can walk on the stormy path.

We'll sing in the moonlight,
Like butterflies in flower valley.
We'll dance in the spotlight,
Like peacock in the rain.

With you I feel safe even in darkness,
In your absence I am lifeless.
Tears in my eyes, each night,
You've gone too far from my sight.

In each drop of blood in my vein,
In each drop of heavenly rain.
I feel your presence,
Even In air I feel your essence.

This is love not leisure,
Some might do it for pleasure.
I know money have all ability,
But I'll love you till the end of infinity.

After full moon, darkness has it's turn,
By this if you got something to learn.
How a small blaze turns a house in flames,
See my soul , not my flaws.

As sweet as melody,
As gloomy as melancholy.
Unaware where I am going,
Solely at a corner dark covering me.

Now I need you the most,
The promises are lost.
Everything looks deserted and quite.
You've gone too far from my sight.

You will get someone better than me,
But my love is eternal,
I'll pray to god to keep you well,
Until and after my funeral.

You were my bright light,
I was wrong you were right,
Tears in my eyes,
You've gone too far from my sight.

Cause You Are Mine

Let me be your moon,
Always there in dark,
Let me be your tune,
Like floral perfumes in a park.

As delicate as jasmine you are,
I'll take your utmost care,
Swans love indicate a sign,
Cause you are mine.

Maybe I am not good in visuals,
For me these are virtual.
I'll love your soul till eternity,
From now till ninety.

I trust you blindly,
But I expect the same from you.
In your up's and down's I'll be there,
Can I expect the same from you?

Love me once, I'll love you twice,
Like stars we will shine, Cause you are mine

Trouble-Maker

You don't know how hard I try,
To hold my tears, try not to cry.
Tired of wearing a fake smile,
Now I am weak but pretend as fine.

Drowning in the lake of tears,
Take me out from this anxiety and fear,
Negative days, Negative nights,
I am losing myself, hold me tight.

Everyone in anguish and tension,
Maybe I am the problem,
And if there is no solution,
So better end the problem.

Hope of Life

There are certain wishes that aren't complete,
There are few dreams that aren't fulfilled.
Still there is a hope to live,
An awesome life.

Raw gold also faces the flames,
And gets beaten by the goldsmith,
To become an expensive jewellery.
Roses also seems so fine,
But it also blooms surrounded by spines.
Still there is a hope to live,
An awesome life.

Condition of today's world is very awful,
Be ready to bite the bullets,
So, never ever give up!
And keep a hope to live,
An awesome life.

In The Lap Of Nature

Relaxing in the green meadow,
Sprawling below the tree's shadow,
Listening to the birds chirping,
Feeling the wind which is blowing.

Admiring the majesty of nature,
She provides her lap to many creatures,
Look! Mother Nature is too kind.
She shares her love and refreshes my mind.

Strong winds making the trees dance,
Ripen fruits falling as now it is the chance,
Fishes moving in the clear brook,
Let's catch them using a rope and hook,

As we are climbing the stairs of technology,
One day nature's beauty will be mythology,
Soon we need to conserve this treasure,
By taking few preventive measures.

Lap of nature is always waiting for thee,
Just plant a tree when you are free.

Celestial Bodies in Night Sky

The pole star glows in
the open sky,
Seems to be like afirefly,
Altogether stars look like a
diamond necklace,
And the full moon shows it's
glowing face.

In the dark night they glare,
But now these moments
are very rare,
They glisten like freshly
fallen snow,
And remove all gloom
and woe.
These celestial bodies
make me glad,
Makes me happy
when I am sad.

Life Like A Corpse

A young traveler exhausted in twisted roads,
Weary of carrying large loads,
For trusting humans he remorse,
A man with life but like a corpse.

A true smile once he had,
And laughed when he was glad,
But now his eyes remains dry,
Because no tears are left to cry.

Painful wounds he endures,
Too young but mentally mature,
Deadly than poison is reality,
He wants to rest till eternity.

Emotions are dead but heart throbs, In
solitude he awfully sobs,
For loving people he remorse,
A man with life but like a corpse.

Last Hours Of Life

Underneath the blue sky,
Knitting some precious memories,
I realized 'life a lie',
Remembering past's lovely stories.

Ending heartbeats I am counting,
Life's last hours are few,
Won't you come for the last meeting,
My eyes are waiting for you.

Holding hands in our youth,
Promises of love that we made,
Feel my hand one last time,
Because my breath seems to fade.

Your love was like a paradise,
Now you'll have to live alone,

A peaceful place above this world,
And body will be buried, burned or thrown.

Life passed learning from mistakes,
When learnt it's too late,
It's your choice to love or hate,
Who knows what's in fate.

Your Love

You are so great,
You are so good.
Dear mother I love you,
When I am hurt,
You cry in pain.
The world is full of thorns,
And you are the golden flower in it,
You are my lovely mother and Papa's wife.

Our Life and Habits

Our life is like a river,
That flows, flows, and flows.
Our life is like an egg,
That can anytime break.

Our bad habits are like heavy stones,
That never move, move, and move.
But it is bad we need to change it soon.
Troubles can come from anywhere in life,
Keep the strength to fight with them,
And a dream to fulfill your aim.

Face or Die

Far from my sweet home,
Aimlessly I just roam.
Wet eyes are my belonging,
Habituated of this sad longing.

Education damands a handsome price,
Standard clothes proves one nice.
In a garden where roses bloom,
Days filled with grief and gloom.

Knots of hope I fasten,
As time passes it gets worsen.
Throat feels my heart throbs,
In lonliness my heart sobs.

Alone and deprived of love,
I miserably need mother's hug.
Circumstances makes a sense certain,
Perhaps I am a burden.

It Hurts

Every finger pointing me,
It's easy to say hard to be.
Believe me I am not bad,
Some harsh words makes me sad.

With me why everyone is so rude,
I am useless, I am not good.
Try to understand me,
At last, I am a human being.

The more I seek for love,
The more hate I get,
It's so sorrowful,
Only thing is to wait.

I say I am fine,
But things are not fine.
Comparison on a beam-balance,
It hurts but prefers silence.

Let The Tears Come Out

Standing all alone in rain,
Neither I can hide nor show the pain.
At last tears rolled down my cheeks,
And again I hide it in the rainy drops.

With zero hope I wait for magic,
But something again happens tragic.
And when you get no shoulder to cry,
Then let the tears come out and dry.

Jokes don't amuse me anymore,
My wet eyes behind the locked door.
When the trees shed their yellow leaves,
But still they wait for those green leaves.

How people live till hundred,
I am tired at fifteen,

Ten reasons to laugh,
Hundred reasons to weep.

Just smile all day like a lie,
Being fake is it fair?
But in this selfish world,
They really don't care.

In the beam-balance of tears and hope,
In the thoughts of neck and rope.
In silence I weep and shout,
Let the tears come out.

You Are My Only One

A special place in my heart,
Just reserved for you,
I'll never let you go apart,
You are my morning dew.
You go away from my grasp,
Like a fistful of sand,
This bond of friendship band.
You mean a lot to me,
But you are so mean.
Don't try to create a mess,
Two options yes or yes,
Let's keep this bond forever fresh.
Our love is so pure,
My pain you are it's cure,
Try to abandon me, I'll kill you for sure.
From this don't try to run,
You may make my fun,
You are my bright sun,

For me do you feel so done?

I need you dear, You are my only one.

Imperfections

I am not perfect,

Yes I am imperfect.

I do little mistakes,

But you are a whole defect.

You might be jealous,

But I am zealous,

I don't pretend to be,

I am good, when I am me.

You just count my flaws,

Rather than checking yourself,

For you a big round of applause,

For you I can't change myself.

Once upon a time,

I used to be decent,

But let me tell you,

I've changed in recent.

Imperfect? no I am perfect,
I am not you puppet.
I love my imperfections,
Not a thing for your satisfaction.

I know you can't bear my happy face,
But you must have heard, "life is a race".
That day I weeped, don't think you won,
The light of my success will be shown.

About me you rumored mean things,
Huh! tried to cut my wings.
Just say what you want to say,
I'll be walking on my way.

The more you'll try to pull me deep,
The more I'll fly high,
Peacefully I'll sleep,
Now it's your turn to cry.

For your sake,
I can't be fake,
I love myself,
The way I am.

I'll do what I want,
I am not your slave,
I'll not lose my dignity,
It's better I'll be in my grave.

Memories

Once you write in page of life,
It can never be erased,
I say I'm fine,
It's a mystery what one have faced.

Smiling all day, But true smile I lack,
Your "good bye" was easy,
The thing which kills are flashbacks.

People have memories with loved ones,
But I never had someone,
Some have gifts, some have diaries,
But my souvenir are memories.

Now memories are preserved,
And time has passed,
I wish I could pause or rewind,

You will be in my mind.

You said you'll leave me never,
Then why you left?
But my heart will love you forever,
That time we spent together.

Can You Hug Me Tight

Be with me for a while,

Gloom hides inside my smile.

Being alone how it feels,

Everyone hurts but no one heals.

If I am not good shall I die,

I know no one will say me good bye.

Pain everyone gives and my heart holds,
The more I tell my feelings,

The more it remains untold.

Can you hug me tight?

In dark nights be my light.

Can you hug me tight?

Until my pain melts in tears.

Can you hug me tight?

And leave me never.

Can you hug me tight?

Until my last breath.

I am feeling blue,

I want to be with you.
If tomorrow I'll not come,
Don't wait for me.
Just enlight a candle,
In my loving memory.

In His Throne Above

The one you love the most,
Leaves you at your worst,
Eyes in which you have trust,
Then greeting "good bye" is a must.

He smile in his throne above,
Things become hard to resolve,
In unexpected journey you get involve,
And this how people evolve.

Your joyous shouts when he hears,
He turns them into tears,
Because your smile he can't bear,
Beloved one's not your near.

How merciless he is?
Just knows how to tease,
Some moments how badly I miss,
Tired body wants to rest in peace.

Broken heart dares to live,
Things changes still I can't believe,
Can you rejuvenate a fallen leaf?
Laughter lost he is the thief.

Burden

Far from my sweet home,
Aimlessly I just roam.
Wet eyes are my belonging,
Habituated of this sad longing.

Education demands a handsome price,
Standard clothes proves one nice.
In a garden where roses bloom,
Days filled with grief and gloom.

Knots of hope I fasten,
As time passes it gets worsen.
Throat feels my heart throbs,
In demands my heart sobs.

Alone and deprived of love,
I miserably need mother's hug.
Circumstances makes a sense certain,
Perhaps I am a burden.

2021

Depression, oppression were my companion,
In winds suffering like a dandelion.
God! Here now it's my turn,
The tragic year 2021.

Countless wounds I suffer,
Dictated it to pen and paper.
God! They made my fun,
The tragic year 2021.

If you think this wasn't fatal,
I was packed off to hostel.
God! Wrap me in your arms,
The tragic year of 2021.

In sarcastic tone they taunted,
Bloody nightmares I was haunted.
No medicine can heal that scar,
Time has gone too far

ANURAG MISHRA

I cried so called me weak,
I laughed so I was a freak.

I regret when I remember,
New hope because it's December.

Hundred Fragments of My Heart

Died flowers between the pages,
Once used to be lively,
Everything burns in outrage,
But our past was lovely.

The pink sky at evening,
Feet dipped in flowing stream,
Fishes touching our skin,
Was it a fantastic dream?

Dark sky with countless sapphires,
Witnessed the oaths of togetherness,
Day dreaming those lovely desires,
Which was not meant to be.

For those moments now I yearn,
Because destiny kept us apart,
Fossilized memories like fern shows,
A hundred fragments of my heart.

Hurt me, Heal me

I felt the warmth of your hands,
And that's how you touched my soul,
I felt the beat of your heart,
But who knows your heart had a hole.

Beneath the glittery night sky,
Entangled hands, I was shy,
Eyes talked for a while,
And I fell in love with your enchanting
smile.

If we could remain like this together,
Throughout life holding hands like lovers.
I want to dive in the valley of love,
But you'll never know the depth of love.

You hurt me then heal me,
I want you to feel me,
In my small world of you and me,
Beside my grave stay with me.

Death

O! The demon of death,
I summon your unholy name,
If life is like a candle,
You must extinguish this flame.

When the last star would perish,
And darkness would reign,
Because invisible scars I cherish,
Which carries the deepest pain.

Shall I plunge from a skyscraper?
To hide my silent scream
Shall I lean on cynide?
To stop my bloody dreams.

.

I planted hope in my heart,
And it died of thirst,
All colours would fade away,
As death is a must.

The Ace of Spades

Facing the face cards,
Queen was chosen by the queen,
And now it became quite intense,
Probably my worthy cards would win.

Gracefully revealing cards of past,
But life is never a game,
How long silent argument would last,
If you lose what a shame.

Eyes don't speak but convey the most,
And wise men says it never lies,
Just a brutal gaze,
Knows how to pacify.

Once you had my heart,
But you torn it into shreds,
You were the tactful queen,
I was the ace of spades.

Old Shoes

I was your old shoes,
Protected you from thorns,
Probably of no use,
Now that I am worn.

Want a place in your heart,
But shoes are for feet,
Covered with pain and dirt,
I think once I used to be neat.

Several pairs now you own,
Branded things as you use,
I am ignored and alone,
But anyone except you I refuse.

New things are kept,
Old stuffs are thrown,
Once you called me mine,
But old shoes are left alone.

Behind A Pretty Smile

Blissful laughter of darkest phase,
Reveals truth of all these days,
Everyone left but melancholy stays,
Escaping from devil's chase.

Lost somewhere in dark woods,
God! Help me to exit,
And if I won't get a ray,
It's better I shall quit.

Every secret remains unknown,
Wounded soul remains alone,
Even rain leads to rainbow,
But life comes with woe.

Pessimistic heart and beautiful eyes,
People admire it for a while,
Mournful thoughts and deepest lies,
Lies behind a pretty smile.

An Ode to Bestfriend

A sparrow flew across the fields,
To tell how my best friend is,
Humming melody as whether is mild,
But coldness makes my heart freeze.

Sweet but shows his apathy,
But he is my favourite companion,
His presence itself is a sympathy,
As he is one in a million.

And if I could just hold his hands,
Throughout autumn and snow,
My life's guardian angel he is,
But he doesn't know.

Completely unaware he is,
As silence seems so fine,
Someday, somewhere he'll know,
This wistful story of mine.

Cherry Blossom

If I could walk beside you,
Blessed with melody of winter,
Above grass dress with few,
Ofcourse my heart would flutter.

Some sandwiches we could have,
Beneath those blissful trees,
In twilight we would walk,
With soothening evening breeze.

Love indeed is mysterious,
In heart when not in sight,
Warm coats are not enough,
In this cold-hearted night.

Your memories are in my heart,
As your company is awesome,
Love is fragrant and pink,
Just like these cherry blossoms.

The Stars Loved the Moon

The moon stares those stars,
Just like I gaze your eyes,
Together we are but still far,
I built love castle upon lies.

I yearn for your voice,
Moon and stars used to talk,
But stars broke and fell apart,
As moonlight touched the sea.

Sea was indeed very beautiful,
And starlight doesn't reached moon,
Alas! stars had faith in love,
But it would be forgotten soon.

How I could withstand the pain,
You are the only one I love,
My envious heart gone insane,
As moonlight touched the sea.

Unrequited Love

The story of the day,
When we sat on last bench,
I wrote all from board,
And you copied my notebook.
Our chaotic classroom was always too loud,
And I came closer to hear you wishper,
Lyrics changed to answers and lectures.
The way you made sure I don't hear,
About your love song and love.
But I know you, I saw your eyes,
The pain, the love for her.
Witnessed you on your lowest days,
Been the reason of your smile,
Yes, you wrote those sweet words for me,
Far from reality, I saw your eyes,
The pain, the love for her...

" Behind A Pretty
Smile lies a deep ocean of
secrets "

www.ingramcontent.com/pod-product-compliance
Lightning Source LLC
LaVergne TN
LVHW010122170826
845678LV00012B/2552

* 9 7 8 8 1 1 9 2 6 2 2 6 7 *